"This Land Is Your Land"
Let's Explore the Southeast

Jill C. Wheeler

Published by Abdo & Daughters, 4940 Viking Drive, Suite 622, Edina, MN 55435.

Library bound edition distributed by Rockbottom Books, Pentagon Tower, P.O. Box 36036, Minneapolis, Minnesota 55435.

Cover Photos by: Bettmann, John Hamilton, AP Worldwide Photos
Inside Photos by: Bettmann Archives: 4, 6, 7, 8, 9, 15, 16, 17, 18, 19
Archive Photos: 4, 7, 10, 11, 15, 19, 20, 21, 22, 23, 24
John Hamilton: 2, 5, 11, 12, 13, 14, 17

Edited by John Hamilton

Library of Congress Cataloging–in–Publication Data
Wheeler, Jill C., 1964-
    The Southeast and Gulf states / Jill C. Wheeler
        p.   cm — (America, this land is your land)
    Includes bibliographical references (p.) and index.
    ISBN 1-56239-296-4
    1. Southern States -- Juvenile literature. 2. Gulf States -- Juvenile literature. [1. Southern States. 2.Gulf States.] I. Title. II. Title: Southeast and Gulf States. III. Series: Wheeler, Jill C., 1964-   America, this land is your land.

F209.3.W48   1994
975—dc20   94-25631
                  CIP
                  AC

Contents

◀ Sunrise on Key
West, Florida.

Let's Explore the Southeast

The Southeast and Gulf States are a land of variety. This area has a rich heritage of agriculture. There are many natural resources like trees, coal, farmland and minerals. Seaports make it easy to send products around the world.

Years ago, the Southeast was very different from the Northeast. The Northeast had many *factories*. People in the Southeast used products made in Northeastern factories. More than half of the people in the Southeast lived on farms. They made their living raising crops and animals. The biggest

▲ The Space Shuttle Discovery blasts off from Cape Canaveral, Florida.

▲ Early settlers in Jamestown, VA.

A heron on the shore of a mangrove swamp.

crop in the Southeast was cotton. Southeast farmers shipped their cotton around the world.

The first people in the Southeast were farmers, too. Native American tribes like the Chickasaw, Cherokee and Creek grew squash, corn, beans, and tobacco.

Today, the Southeast has its own industries. Factories make furniture, textiles and paper. Computer and services companies are busy. The mild climate and warm sunshine attract many tourists.

The first visitors to the Southeast were from Europe. A Spanish man named Juan Ponce de Leon visited the place we call Florida in 1513.

Later, another Spanish man explored the Southeast. His name was Hernando de Soto. He was looking for gold. He was the first European to see the Mississippi River.

The Southeast and Gulf States have gone through many changes since then. One was the American Civil War. Southern farmers relied on African *slaves* to help them. Many people in the Northeast believed slavery should be against the law. One reason the North and South fought the Civil War was over slavery.

Many other historic events took place in the Southeast and Gulf States. We'll look at more in the next chapter.

Historical Highlights

The history of the Southeast and Gulf States is as colorful as the landscape. It includes tales of daring explorers and peaceful farmers. It was a place of power struggles among foreign nations. Soldiers fought some of the nation's worst battles on its lands. Here is a look at the events that shaped this land:

▲ *Union and Confederate troops fight during the United States Civil War.*

1513 Spanish explorer Juan Ponce de Leon leaves Puerto Rico. He is looking for the mythical *Fountain of Youth*. He finds a new land and names it Florida.

1539-1542 Another Spanish explorer, Hernando de Soto, lands in Florida. He explores modern-day Alabama, Mississippi, Florida, Georgia and part of Texas.

1565 Settlers found St. Augustine, Florida. It is the first permanent European settlement in the Southeast.

1585 English settlers found a colony at Roanoke Island. The island is off the coast of North Carolina.

1607 A group of English settlers found Jamestown in Virginia. They hope to find gold there.

1619 The first African slaves arrive in Jamestown, Virginia.

1663 The King of England gives a large piece of land to eight noblemen. Part of this land becomes North and South Carolina.

1682 French explorer Rene Robert Cavelier, Sieur de La Salle paddles down the Mississippi River in birchbark canoes. He and his men build three forts along the way. La Salle claims the land along the Mississippi for France.

1693 The College of William and Mary is founded in Williamsburg, Virginia.

1754-1763 France and England fight the French and Indian War. The war is for control of the new continent. England wins the war. France gives up much of its land.

1775 The Revolutionary War begins. The colonies of Virginia, Georgia, North Carolina, and South Carolina join the fight against England.

◀ *Ponce De Leon searches for the Fountain of Youth.*

▼ *A Mississippi cotton plantation in 1954.*

1783 Settlers create the United States of America.

1788 Georgia becomes the fourth state in the new country. South Carolina is eighth. Virginia is 10th.

1789 North Carolina becomes a state. George Washington becomes the nation's first president.

1793 Eli Whitney invents the cotton gin. People can clean fifty times as much cotton with this machine as they could by hand.

1803 The United States buys the Louisiana Territory from France.

1812 Louisiana becomes the thirteenth state.

1813 Americans take control of Alabama.

1817 The government divides Mississippi Territory. This creates Alabama Territory. Mississippi becomes the 20th state.

1819 Alabama joins the Union as the 22nd state. The United States signs a treaty with Spain. The treaty gives the new nation the land of Florida.

1822 Congress creates Florida Territory.

1838-1839 The United States Government forces 16,000 Cherokee people from their homes. They march them

to *reservations* in Oklahoma. A quarter of the people die along the way. They call their route the Trail of Tears.

1836 American settlers in Texas declare independence from Mexico. A Mexican leader kills 187 settlers in a battle at the Alamo.

1845 Florida becomes the 27th state. The United States annexes Texas. Texas becomes the 28th state.

1859 John Brown raids the federal *arsenal* at Harper's Ferry. He wants to end slavery.

1860 Voters elect President Abraham Lincoln. Lincoln wants to outlaw slavery. South Carolina *secedes* from the *Union*.

1861 Six more states secede from the Union. They form a separate country. They call it the *Confederate States of America*.

1861 Confederate soldiers fire on Fort Sumter in South Carolina. The American Civil War begins.

1862 Union ships capture New Orleans.

1863 President Lincoln says slaves in the Confederate states are free. The government calls this the Emancipation Proclamation.

1863 Union troops defeat Confederate forces at Gettysburg, Pennsylvania.

1864 Union General William Sherman begins a march through the Southeast.

◀ *Cherokee Native Americans on the Trail of Tears.*

◀ *American settlers fight the Mexican Army during the battle for the Alamo in Texas, 1836.*

1865 Confederate leader Robert E. Lee *surrenders* to Union leader Ulysses Grant. The surrender is at Appomattox, Virginia. The Civil War ends.

1865 The *Reconstruction* begins. The Union tries to help Southern states repair damage from the war.

1866 Congress passes the Fourteenth Amendment. This gives rights to African-Americans. The federal government begins forcing Southern states to pass this amendment.

1868 Alabama, Florida, Louisiana, and North Carolina rejoin the Union.

1870 Georgia, Mississippi, Virginia, and Texas rejoin the Union.

1877 Northern troops leave the last of the old Confederate states. The Reconstruction ends.

1901 Prospectors discover oil in Louisiana.

1903 The Wright Brothers make the first airplane flight at Kitty Hawk, North Carolina.

1912 The first train reaches Florida's Key West. It travels over a series of bridges built from island to island.

1919 Residents found Miami Beach. It becomes a tourist attraction.

1956 A court orders Montgomery, Alabama, to *desegregate* its schools. This means all schools must teach both black and white children.

1958 The United States launches its first *satellite* from Cape Canaveral, Florida.

1962 John Glenn becomes the first American in space. His rocket leaves from Cape Canaveral. Cape Canaveral later becomes Cape Kennedy.

1963 An *assassin* kills President John F. Kennedy in Dallas, Texas. Texan Lyndon Johnson becomes President of the United States.

1973 Atlanta voters elect Maynard Jackson mayor. He is the first African-American mayor in a large Southern city.

1977 Georgia native Jimmy Carter becomes President of the United States.

1981 The space shuttle Columbia takes its first flight. It leaves from Cape Canaveral, Florida.

1992 Hurricane Andrew hits Florida and parts of the Gulf Coast. The storm leaves thousands of people homeless.

The Lay of the Land

The land of the Southeast varies as much as the people. Some lands are low and flat. Others are gently rolling. Wooded mountains and deep valleys cover some places. Visitors find swamps and deserts in others.

Much of the Southeast is a region called the Coastal Plain. It runs along the Atlantic Coast and the Gulf of Mexico. The land near the water is low and flat. There are many sandy beaches. Other areas are *swamps* or *marshes*. The land in the Coastal Plain is rich and fertile. Farmers grow crops such as corn, tobacco and peanuts here.

▼ *Shenandoah National Park in Virginia.*

▲ *Hardwood hammocks dot the vast Florida Everglades.*

Cypress Gardens in Charleston, South ▶ *Carolina.*

The Southeast also has many broad rivers. The mighty Mississippi flows to the sea here. The land along these rivers is very rich. It is good for growing cotton. Along the rivers and lakes are swamps. Slow-moving bodies of water drain these swamps. These bodies are *bayous*.

North of the Coastal Plain are the Appalachian Highlands. This land has mountains, plateaus and valleys. The plateaus have good farm land. Farmers here grow cotton and tobacco. The mountains are the highest in the Southeast.

Many rivers flow from the plateaus to the Coastal Plain. The border

between these two areas is the Fall Line. There are many rapids and waterfalls along this line. This is because the water in the rivers falls from high areas to lower areas. The falls and rapids of the Fall Line stopped many settlers. They stopped near the Fall Line instead of crossing it. Later, they learned how to use the falls to generate electric power.

The land changes dramatically farther west. West Texas is a land of sandy hills and dry plains.

Some of the natural wonders in the Southeast and Gulf States are:

▲ *Boats sail the warm waters of the Gulf of Mexico.*

The Blue Ridge Mountains include the highest points in the Southeast. Some peaks are more than 6,000 feet above sea level. Thick forests cover these beautiful mountains. The Blue Ridge Mountains include the Great Smoky and Black Mountain chains.

Okefenokee Swamp is a giant swamp in Georgia. It extends into Florida. It is a wilderness area. The Suwannee River forms the swamp.

The Florida Everglades is a large, swampy grasslands area in southern Florida. It is one of the nation's largest national parks. It covers more than 5,000 square miles. The Everglades is home to many unusual animals.

Big Cypress Swamp also is in southern Florida. Visitors can see many unusual plants and animals here.

Lake Okeechobee in southern Florida covers 700 square miles. It is the second largest natural lake located completely in the United States.

The Mississippi Delta is south of New Orleans. It is where the Mississippi empties into the Gulf of Mexico. *Silt* carried down the river forms the Delta.

De Soto Caverns in Alabama is a network of onyx caves. Native Americans used the caves for a burial ground. Later, Confederate soldiers used them to mine gunpowder. The caverns include a 12-story-high chamber.

The Florida Keys are a chain of islands. They stretch 200 miles from the tip of Florida. The Overseas Highway connects the islands. The farthest island is Key West. Key West is the southernmost point in the United States.

▼ *An aerial view of Key West, Florida, the southernmost point in the United States.*

13

Plants & Animals

The Southeast and Gulf States are home to many unusual plants and animals. This is because some of the land is in a *tropical* climate.

Florida has some of the most unusual animals. Alligators live in the Everglades. Alligators may grow to be 18 feet long. They have sharp teeth and strong jaws.

Another Everglades resident is the kite. A kite is a type of hawk. It eats water snails. It uses its hooked bill to catch the snails. The kite has been in danger in recent years. As people drain the swamps, it has fewer places to live. Other common birds are the wood stork, the mockingbird, and the egret.

▲ *A snowy egret hunting for fish.*
▼ *An alligator basking on shore.*

The Southeast and Gulf States have many animals common to North America. Deer, skunks, wild turkeys, raccoons and bobcats live there. Other residents are not so common. Bobcats and mountain lions live in some areas. Armadillos and wild boars scurry through wooded areas. In

◄ Cotton plant.

▲ *Raccoons.*

marshlands you can see beautiful pink flamingos, pelicans and scaly loggerhead turtles. The loggerhead is the largest sea turtle. It can weigh up to 1,500 pounds.

Throughout the Southeast and Gulf States, heavy rainfall creates lush vegetation. Colorful camellias, azaleas, poinsettias and lilies decorate gardens. Spanish moss drapes magnolia trees. The mild weather leaves the landscape green all year.

In the swamplands, you'll see water lilies and sawgrass marshes. Swamplands also are home to ferns and the unusual Venus's-flytrap plant. The plant's tip attracts and catches insects for the plant to eat. Tropical mangrove trees grow in groves in shallow saltwater.

The warm weather also lets farmers grow special crops. Many oranges and grapefruit come from the Southeast and Gulf States. Cotton and sugar cane are grown here, too.

Marine life thrives off the Gulf Coast. Divers look for sponges. People dry the sponges and use them for many tasks. Fishers gather shrimp, crawfish, tuna and marlin. Rivers and swamplands are home to trout, catfish and black crappies.

A mother ► flamingo and its chick.

Famous Folks

Henry Lewis "Hank" Aaron
(1934-) Aaron is one of the
world's great baseball batters. He
was born in Mobile, Alabama. In
1974, he broke Babe Ruth's home
run record. He hit more than 755
home runs in his career.

Joe Louis (1914-1981) Louis was
one of America's greatest boxers.
He defended the World Heavy-
weight title 25 times. He was from
Lexington, Alabama.

Willie Howard Mays, Jr. (1931-)
Mays was voted baseball player of
the decade for 1960-69. Born in
Fairfield, Alabama, he was a tal-
ented fielder, batter and base run-
ner.

Jesse Owens (1913-1980) Owens
was an outstanding track and field
athlete. He won four gold medals at
the 1936 Olympics. He was born in
Danville, Alabama.

Osceola (1804?-1838) Osceola
was a leader in the Seminole tribe.
He was born in Georgia. He led the
Seminoles in fighting the white
settlers. Soldiers later captured him
and he died in prison.

Tyrus Raymond "Ty" Cobb
(1886-1961) This famous baseball
player was born in Narrows, Georgia. He joined the Baseball Hall of
Fame in 1936.

Louis Daniel Armstrong (1900-
1971) Armstrong was born in New
Orleans, Louisiana. He played the
trumpet and led a band. He became
a famous jazz musician.

 **Martin Luther King, Jr.** (1929-1968) King was born in Atlanta, Georgia. He was the son of a minister and became a minister, too. He helped African-Americans fight for equal rights with white people. An assassin killed him in 1968.

Margaret Mitchell (1900-1949) Mitchell wrote "Gone With the Wind." It won a Pulitzer prize and was made into a movie. She was born in Atlanta, Georgia.

Jack Roosevelt "Jackie" Robinson (1919-1972) Robinson was the first black athlete to play major league baseball. He was from Cairo, Georgia. He helped other black athletes find acceptance in professional sports.

Jefferson Davis (1808-1889) Davis became president of the Confederate States in 1861. He was born in Fairview, Mississippi. After the Civil War, he spent two years in prison.

Thomas Jonathan "Stonewall" Jackson (1824-1863) Jackson was a Confederate general. His stand at the Battle of Bull Run earned him the nickname "Stonewall." He was from Clarksburg, West Virginia.

Jimmy Carter (1924-) Carter became president of the United States in 1976. Before that, he was Governor of Georgia. He was born in Plains, Georgia. He became known for his work in civil and human rights.

Tennessee Williams (1911-1983) Williams was born in Columbus, Mississippi. He was the son of a traveling salesman. He won two Pulitzer prizes for plays he wrote. He also wrote poetry.

Andrew Jackson (1767-1845) Jackson was the seventh president of the United States. He was from Waxhaw, South Carolina. Before becoming president, he was a military leader.

Joan Crawford (1906-1977) This Hollywood actress started her career as a chorus girl. She was from San Antonio, Texas. She starred in many movies.

Chester William Nimitz (1885-1966) Nimitz was a naval commander. He helped defeat Japan during World War II. He was a native of Fredericksburg, Texas.

Elvis Presley (1935-1977) Presley was the most popular performer in the United States by 1956. He began singing in his church choir. He taught himself to play guitar. He was born in Tupelo, Mississippi.

William Faulkner (1897-1962) Faulkner was a Pulitzer-prize winning author. He often set stories in his native Mississippi.

Thomas Jefferson (1743-1826) Jefferson was the nation's third president. He helped write the *Declaration of Independence.*

He was born in Albemarle County, Virginia.

Robert Edward Lee (1807-1870) General Lee led Confederate soldiers during the Civil War. He was born in Westmoreland County, Virginia. He was a popular and skilled leader.

Cyrus Hall McCormick (1809-1884) This inventor was born in Rockbridge County, Virginia. He invented a reaper to help farmers harvest grain. He formed a farm equipment company.

 **Helen Keller** (1880-1968) Keller was born blind and deaf in Tuscumbia, Alabama. She learned to speak and write anyway. She devoted her life to helping people with disabilities.

George C. Scott (1927-) This actor is from Wise, West Virginia. He has starred in movies, TV shows and on stage. He refused an Oscar for his role in the movie "Patton."

Pocahontas (1595-1617) Pocahontas was a Native American woman. She saved the life of an English settler. She was born near Jamestown, Virginia.

Favorite Cities

New Orleans

New Orleans, Louisiana, hosts the Mardi Gras each year. This celebration takes place just before Lent. The city sits on the Mississippi River. To the north is giant saltwater Lake Pontchartrain. It was once part of the Gulf of Mexico.

New Orleans is the state's largest city. It features a diverse population. Cultural influences are from France, Italy, Spain and Cuba. The city has one of the world's largest ports. Tourism, food processing and chemical industries are important for the economy.

New Orleans' Superdome attracts many sporting events each year. Tulane, Loyola and Dillard Universities are there. Many people visit the French Quarter. The French Quarter has many unique buildings. Jazz music began in New Orleans.

▲ *Fancy grillwork decorates many buildings in New Orleans' French Quarter.*

Settlers founded the city in 1718. They named it for the *regent* of France. His name was Phillippe II, duc d'Orleans. The United States bought the city as part of the *Louisiana Purchase* in 1803. In 1862, the Confederate city fell to the Union navy.

Dallas

Dallas, Texas, is the second-largest city in Texas. It sits on the Trinity River. The city grew up because it was on an easy spot for crossing the river.

Major businesses in Dallas include insurance and financial companies. There are many corporate headquarters, too. Factories make aero-

space goods, plus electronics, processed foods and clothing.

Dallas has many excellent schools. These include Southern Methodist University and the University of Dallas. The city is home to the Cotton Bowl.

A settler built the first home in Dallas in 1841. Residents named the city for United States Vice President George Miflin Dallas. Confederate troops used Dallas for supplies during the Civil War.

Prospectors discovered oil in Texas in 1930. This spurred the city's growth. In 1963, Dallas saw the assassination of President John F.

▲ *A skyline view of Dallas, Texas.*

Kennedy. The city now has an exhibit on the event for visitors.

Atlanta

Atlanta, Georgia, is the transportation, commercial and financial center of the Southeast. It grew up around a railroad from Chattanooga, Tennessee. Today, the city has many factories. The factories manufacture goods from cars to planes and soft drinks.

Atlanta is home to the Georgia Institute of Technology and Emory University. Cultural attractions include a symphony and the Atlanta College of Art. Tourists can

◀Central City Park in Atlanta, Georgia.

visit the Martin Luther King, Jr. National Historic Site.

Atlanta began in 1821. Creek Indians gave land to the state of Georgia. During the Civil War, Atlanta was a Confederate supply station. Union forces occupied the city in 1864. The city burned in November of that year.

Atlanta has come a long way since the fires of the Civil War. In 1996, it will host the Olympic summer games.

Charleston

Charleston, South Carolina, is the oldest city in the state. It is a major Atlantic Coast port. Factories in the city make fertilizer, paper, chemicals and textiles. The city's harbor makes it easy to ship these products around the world.

City attractions include a U.S. Naval base and the Citadel. The Citadel is a military college. The city's many historic buildings attract many tourists.

Settlers began Charleston in 1670 at Albemarle Point. They called it Charles Towne after King Charles II. The city moved to its present location in 1680. Charleston's Fort Sumter was where the Civil War began. In 1886, a terrible earthquake hit the city. In 1989, Hurricane Hugo damaged Charleston.

▲ *Richmond, the capital of Virginia.*

Richmond

Richmond, Virginia, is the capital of Virginia. It is on the James River near the Atlantic Ocean. The city's port, railroads and highways have made it an important site. Its industries include tobacco processing and chemical manufacturing.

Visitors to Richmond can see the state capitol designed by Thomas Jefferson. Saint John's Episcopal Church also is here. Patriot Patrick Henry made a famous speech in the church. In the speech, he called for "liberty or death." The Confederate White House also is in Richmond.

Richmond was one of the first cities in the United States. Settlers came to the area around Richmond in 1607. British soldiers attacked the city in 1781.

During the Civil War, many battles took place near Richmond. Union General Ulysses Grant took control of the city in 1865. Much of it later burned.

Miami

▲ *Sunbathers in Miami, Florida.*

Miami, Florida, is the second-largest city in Florida. It sits on beautiful Biscayne Bay. The city has many cultural influences. These include large Hispanic and African-American communities.

Miami is one of the nation's favorite tourist sites. It has professional baseball, basketball and football teams. Each year, the city hosts the Orange Bowl. In addition to tourism, Miami has many factories. The factories make cement, plastics, electronic parts and clothing.

Miami began as a Spanish settlement in the 1560s. The city grew quickly after 1895. That year, Henry Flagler began developing it as a resort area. The growth boom continued in the 1920s and 1950s.

Miami has been a destination for many immigrants. People flocked to Miami from Cuba and Haiti in recent years.

Fast Facts

Alabama

Population: 4 million
Area: 51,705 square miles
Capital: Montgomery
Industries: Agriculture, apparel, chemicals, electronics, manufacturing, paper.
State Flower: Camellia
State Bird: Yellowhammer
Statehood Date: December 14, 1819

Florida

Population: 12.9 million
Area: 58,664 square miles
Capital: Tallahassee
Industries: Agriculture, electronics, manufacturing, printing, tourism.
State Flower: Orange blossom
State Bird: Mockingbird
Statehood Date: March 3, 1845

Georgia

Population: 6.4 million
Area: 58,910 square miles
Capital: Atlanta
Industries: Agriculture, chemical products, forestry, manufacturing, tourism.
State Flower: Cherokee rose
State Bird: Brown thrasher
Statehood Date: January 2, 1788

Louisiana

Population: 4.2 million
Area: 47,752 square miles
Capital: Baton Rouge
Industries: Agriculture, chemicals, construction, electronics, manufacturing, mining, transportation.
State Flower: Magnolia
State Bird: Eastern brown pelican
Statehood Date: April 30, 1812

Mississippi

Population: 2.6 million
Area: 47,689 square miles
Capital: Jackson
Industries: Agriculture, manufacturing, seafood, shipping, timber.
State Flower: Magnolia
State Bird: Mockingbird
Statehood Date: Dec. 10, 1817

North Carolina

Population: 6.6 million
Area: 52, 669 square miles
Capital: Raleigh
Industries: Agriculture, manufacturing, tourism.
State Flower: Dogwood
State Bird: Cardinal
Statehood Date: Nov. 21, 1789

South Carolina

Population: 3.5 million
Area: 31,113 square miles
Capital: Columbia
Industries: Agriculture, chemical products, manufacturing, timber, textiles, tourism.
State Flower: Yellow jessamine
State Bird: Carolina wren
Statehood Date: May 23, 1788

Texas

Population: 17 million
Area: 266,807 square miles
Capital: Austin
Industries: Aerospace, cattle, cotton, electrical machinery, manufacturing, oil.
State Flower: Bluebonnet
State Bird: Mockingbird
Statehood Date: Dec. 29, 1845

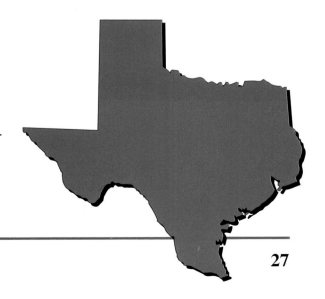

Virginia

Population: 6.1 million
Area: 40,767 square miles
Capital: Richmond
Industries: Agriculture, manufacturing, research, technology, tourism.
State Flower: Dogwood
State Bird: Cardinal
Statehood Date: June 25, 1788

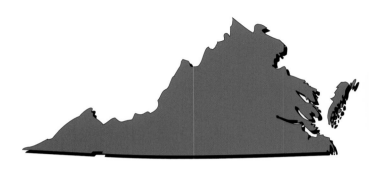

West Virginia

Population: 1.8 million
Area: 24,232 square miles
Capital: Charleston
Industries: Agriculture, manufacturing, mining, tourism.
State Flower: Big rhododendron
State Bird: Cardinal
Statehood Date: June 20, 1863

Suggestions For Further Reading

Kids Learn America by Patricia Gordon and Reed C. Snow, Williamsburg Publishing Co.

Children's Atlas of the United States, Rand McNally & Company.

All About Our 50 States by Margaret Ronan, Random House.

The South by Jerry Jennings, The Fideler Company.

Let's Discover the States: The South by Thomas G. Aylesworth and Virginia L. Aylesworth, Chelsea House Publishers.

The Civil War by Alden R. Carter, Franklin Watts.

The Trail of Tears by R. Conrad Stein, Childrens Press.

A Kid's Guide to Florida, by Karen Grove, Gulliver Books, Harcourt Brace Jovanovich.

Glossary

Arsenal
A place where people store guns and other weapons.

Assassin
A person who kills another person.

Bayou
A shallow, slow-moving creek or stream.

Confederate States of America
Eleven Southern states that formed their own country and fought against Northern states in the Civil War.

Declaration of Independence
A document colonial leaders wrote. It demanded their freedom from England.

Desegregate
To stop people from being separated because of their race.

Fountain of Youth
A mythical place. People who drank water from the fountain would never get old.

Louisiana Purchase
A large territory west of the Mississippi River. The United States bought the land from France in 1803.

Marsh
Soft, wet land.

Reconstruction
The 12 years after the Civil War. The North helped rebuild the South during these years.

Regent
A person who rules for another person.

Reservation
A place where the government sent Native Americans to live.

Satellite
A rocket-like object put into space.

Secede
To withdraw from something.

Silt
Fine pieces of soil that float in water.

Slave
A person forced to work for another person. Slave owners considered their slaves property.

Swamp
Wet, spongy land.

Technologies
Using science to solve a particular problem.

Tropical
Warm, moist weather.

Union
Name given to the Northern states during the United States Civil War.

Index